# The Wednesday Lady

Beyond the ABCs
One teacher's memories revealed in report
card comments, letters, and recollections.

Ellen Lewis

The Wednesday Lady

*Beyond the ABCs*
*One teacher's memories revealed in report card comments, letters, and recollections.*

Copyright© 2023 by Ellen Parker Lewis
All rights reserved.

Published by Rebel Books Press, LLC Trust the Signs is a work of nonfiction. Names have been changed in this work of nonfiction.

Cover design by Diane Lilli
First Edition
November 2023
ISBN 979-8-8689-7818-0

To learn more visit:
Rebel Books Press, LLC
https://rebelbookspress.com/

## Dedication

This book is dedicated to my son Dan, Barbara Hirsch, Martin Parker, Eleanor Marotta, Nell Burgeson, my dog Rummy, and all the students whose lives I have touched and who have taught me more than I ever could have imagined over the past 50 years.

## Foreword

## Every Story Begins with Once Upon a Time

Once upon a time there was a maiden whose personal fairy tale had been unexpectedly interrupted. Her mother insisted upon placing an inquiry in the town crier's list of announcements seeking a reference for someone who was proficient in casting magic spells. Hopefully, the request for help would spark the curiosity of a talented individual who could reverse the tragic circumstances and turn them to favor the grieving young maiden.

"That beguiling little elf, Rumple somebody or other might be available. Such a tricky little whippersnapper must have a long list of successes on his resume," thought the damsel's mother.

In addition, there had been some gossip in the village, about the fairy godmother, who used her magical powers to change a scrub girl like Cinderella into a princess. Rumor had it that this fairy godmother had recently moved into a senior citizen community nearby.

"There must be a way to contact the elderly woman!" our damsel's mom concluded.

But luck was not on the side of our young maiden. There were no responses to the town crier's requests for help and the elderly fairy godmother was never located. The wedding date passed without a wedding.

No one would have ever dreamed that this kind-hearted fair maiden would suffer the unimaginable, the humiliation, of announcing the cancellation of her nuptials to one of the most eligible lads living in the tri-kingdom area.

Unbeknownst to the maiden, her Prince Charming had been promised by his family to the daughter of a wealthy businessman, whose family lived in a fancy palace unlike the modest dwelling in which our damsel was raised.

His parents believed that marrying into the right family would further enhance the prince's opportunities for future success. The prince declared his love for our young maiden and tried untangling the strings that tied him to his parents' commitments, but in the end the obligations outweighed his efforts.

Hours of sorrow-filled contemplation turned into days of despair for the saddened damsel. Days became weeks. The wedding had been set for late August. Three long months went by as she thought and rethought her options. Almost all her friends were married. They knew who they were, "Mrs. I'm Married." But without a husband how would she define herself?

As the days began ushering in the cold winds of the upcoming winter, both the young maiden and her mother began to accept the fact that there would be no little elves and no fairy godmothers who would magically appear and instantly manufacture a happy ending.

Finally, the saddened mother realized it was up to her to do something.

She ordered a catalog from the kingdom's university.

When it arrived, she presented it to her daughter.

"Enough of this self-pity. Look through this catalog to see which of the graduate schools will be accepting candidates for the spring semester," she suggested.

Only one of the graduate programs was accepting January admissions.

Our young maiden applied and was accepted to the Graduate School of Education.

She had never thought about becoming a teacher. Mostly she had thought about becoming a "Mrs. Somebody." That is what her family had taught her and that is what society expected of her.

After two years of study, she graduated and got a job in a small-town teaching first grade.

It did not take much time before she realized that there were many ways to define herself other than becoming "Mrs. Somebody."

She went on to teach for decades, winning the hearts of countless young children and lovingly referred to as "The Wednesday Lady" by some of the many students she taught each week.

Along the way she kept accurate letters that she had sent to colleagues, children, and parents.

This is her true story.

And she lived - and lives - happily ever after!

**After happily ever after ...**

Living happily ever after does not mean that life continues with no setbacks and no false illusions. Experiences in the classroom with students is challenging and rewarding. Dealing with the people who run the bureaucratic machine that determines and sets the environment for teaching to take place are often ignorant of their own errors in judgement, as well as how the impact of their decisions can become counterintuitive to the job teachers are trying to do.

Hopefully by sharing my fairy tale as a teacher, the reader gathers a perspective that bad things happen and that the world can be a scary place, but that happy endings do exist, and that acknowledging that truth can make us all a little braver in real life.

Fairy tales may provide some models of bravery which offer examples that can be applied in our own lives to help getting through the rough spots.

Although I am plagued with the saddest of my stories, the sweetest memories in the classroom provide some of the greatest joys of my life.

## Part I

There will be laughter.

# Chapter 1

## The Wednesday Lady

During the covid pandemic I was contacted by a teacher with whom I had taught in the past, asking me if I was interested in a part-time position. The job entailed working with students in nonpublic schools who needed extra reinforcement in the areas of math and literacy. At times I would be working with students in the classroom. Other assignments would require teaching virtual lessons to students via Zoom.

After I began this job as a "traveling educational troubadour" I found that most teachers were eager for me to become part of their academic team. But there were and are others, who perceive my presence as that of a threat, a snoop, an annoyance, or an interloper.

When I was a classroom teacher, I welcomed the help from teachers who were hired to provide supplemental instruction. That extra bit of explanation, practice, or clarification can often be the missing component to help a student to succeed. But I understand that not all teachers agree.

For me, this new job offered an opportunity to do something I found both challenging and rewarding during unprecedented times.

Once the pandemic subsided, the virtual lessons were discontinued, and I met with students at assigned schools in areas designated by the school's administration.

Over the past several years I have begun to acknowledge that I have learned as many lessons as I have taught.

I continue to feel fortunate to have this experience at a time when others have long since left their careers behind.

For example, one day last year, after arriving at one of my assigned schools, I was approached by the principal. She asked to speak with me before beginning my lessons for that day.

I felt a bit apprehensive and quickly searched my memory for any recent unusual occurrences or difficulties that might be the cause for this unscheduled meeting.

I could think of none.

Within minutes after I had assembled the materials for my first class, the principal opened the door of the library, which was my designated teaching area. As she walked in my direction with a huge smile on her face, I immediately felt relieved!

"I am not sure," she began, "that you are aware of the fact that we have welcomed many visitors who are both religious and secular members of the community to our school over the past decade."

"But," she continued," None of these honored and distinguished visitors has ever received the welcome that you receive each Wednesday afternoon."

"And neither Gilda the director of this school nor I as the principal have ever been the recipient of the greeting you receive each week."

"You see," she announced," when the students who are on their lunch break at that time, get the first glimpse of your car pulling into the parking lot, they gather and form a cluster by the window.

"Then they begin their Wednesday afternoon ritual starting with rhythmically clapping their hands and begin to chant in unison: 'The Wednesdays Lady's Here. …. The Wednesdays Lady's Here!"

"You must be special to have endeared yourself to our community of children, " she concluded. "To receive a standing ovation each week when you arrive is surely a tribute to who you are! I want you to know how much we appreciate all that you do for all our students!"

## Chapter 2

## The Report Card Comments

The 1960's represented a time of challenge and change. It was a time to rethink and restructure the foundations on which our country was built.

Amidst the turmoil and chaos, and in the shadows of a political revolution and an evolution, the seeds of equality and accountability were planted and began to grow.

While mankind took that giant leap on the moon and while young women were putting on miniskirts and taking off their bras, a 16-year-old sophomore in high school was struggling with his own demons, academic ones. He was plagued by the words written on his report card."

"Paul is an enigma. He is apparently quite intelligent. Yet he struggles to utilize and apply the knowledge presented in class. This issue in combination with a lack of enthusiasm suggest a rather bleak future."

Today Dr. Paul is in his 42nd year as a family physician but remains haunted by the words written decades ago.

How many adults can still recall the sting of a teacher's poorly chosen words? Yet there are others with positive experiences and who can attribute personal success to a teacher or mentor?

What about you? Are words of a demeaning nature that a teacher once used to describe you still haunting you? Can you hear the echoes of descriptions of you whether written or spoken?

Or are you among the more fortunate who were blessed with having had a teacher who recognized your strengths instead of emphasizing your weaknesses. Perhaps you met a teacher who inspired and nurtured you somewhere along the way?

Join me as I share my journey which encompasses my five decades in the classroom, a compilation of recollections, comments, and circumstances which "tell it all."

Hopefully the series of vignettes I have compiled will offer a glimpse into a world of triumph and failure, of joy and frustration as experiences by all involved. And my goal is that after turning the last page you will consider my journey to have been one that was worthy of my efforts.

My name is Ellen Lewis. This past school year was the 50th anniversary of my first class. It marked their fiftieth year since being together in my first-grade classroom.

At the present time, I am back in the classroom, after a short hiatus.

I am employed part time by the New Jersey Educational Services Commission as a compensatory education teacher.

I may be referred to by my students as: Ms. Lewis, Miss Ellen, Mrs. Lewis, the Candy Lady, or the Wednesday Lady. But whatever they choose to call me, they know that there will always be a song to sing and dance to, a poem or a story to spur their imagination, a game to play, a project to create and some jokes to share.

Twenty years ago, when I joined my first writers' group, someone asked me to summarize the kinds of writing I had done. My answer was succinct: "Grocery lists and report card comments."

Each section of my book will share intimate moments between myself, my students, my colleagues and/or the parents of children I taught in school.

Looking back on decades of teaching, I discovered there are quite a few surreal real-life events that took place, along with bittersweet family troubles and very funny letters that may seem familiar to my fellow educators.

If you are a teacher, I highly recommend keeping a detailed diary of your most memorable classroom moments, from the hilarious to the tragic to the sublime.

In 1972 I graduated with a master's degree in education from Rutgers University in New Brunswick, New Jersey. Most of my fellow graduate students were not even getting interviews, and so I felt fortunate and honored that I was offered a teaching position in two different school districts.

My student teaching experience was with a cooperating teacher who was well known and revered in the city of New Brunswick. Receiving an "A" for my performance in the classroom, as well as her letters of recommendation, opened the door for me, along with the "A" I received on the master's exam and a GPA of a solid "A" for course work.

At the end of my student teaching assignment, my advisor from the School of Education at Rutgers was invited into the classroom to observe a lesson I had planned for his evaluation.

I was not expecting my cooperating teacher's remarks, and by the look on his face, neither did the distinguished professor.

"I am assuming," she began, "that we both agree that Miss Parker has earned an "A" for her student teaching experience."

Then she added, "But if by some chance her grade does not reflect her excellent performance, I will use my influence to make sure that you, Professor K., will never again participate in the teacher training process at Rutgers University!"

I was one of the few to receive offers from two different school districts for full-time positions. It took me a great deal of thought but I accepted the job offer with the smaller and lower paying school district. After signing my contract, I suddenly realized I was still very much a novice who wasn't really prepared to figure out where and how to begin my journey with the twenty-eight six and seven-year-old students, who had been assigned to my class for the next one hundred and eighty days.

Even after hours of note taking at lectures and reading the latest theories on learning and having the opportunity of having the model lessons of a veteran educator to reflect upon, I wasn't quite sure how to put all the information together to be successful on my own in the classroom.

The year 1972 was synonymous with change, not just for me, but also for the world.

An unpopular and divisive war was raging halfway around the world.

The intellectuals in academia were leading a coalition to impeach the President of the United States due to a scandal entitled, "Watergate!"

Women's voices were finally being heard and Congress was being confronted with issues which had never been discussed before, like equal rights for blacks. The Supreme Court had also started discussing issues like a woman's right to choose.

I was among those pleased to discover that "professional" women were beginning to be able to make the choice of wearing pants to work!

It was during this chaos that I began trying to unlock the keys to building a successful career by educating six and seven-year-olds. I had never initiated or organized my own plan to provide the first step of a solid foundation required to enable these young students to establish a sturdy foundation for their academic future.

How lucky was I to become informally mentored by two master teachers, Eleanor Marotta and Nell Burgeson, who took me under their talented wings and opened my eyes and heart to the joys and struggles of becoming successful at nurturing young children and preparing them for their academic and social futures.

I had never realized or understood the responsibility of the job until my two mentors demonstrated the importance of what we did each day.

Many of my colleagues spent decades by my side while others did not have the stamina or the desire for commitment.

Despite my age I find myself still drawn to the classroom to contribute whatever I can.

Recently while working with two third graders, I overheard one boy talking to his fellow classmate.

"Danny, do you realize what kinds of memories we are building each time we get to work with Miss Ellen?"

I quietly walked away, pretending not to hear what the young boy said, and had to use my sleeve to wipe tears from my eyes.

To all of my fellow educators: if you are working hard at your job in the classroom, with a positive open spirit, then remember these words, because they also belong to you.

I hope you enjoy "The Wednesday Lady."

## Chapter 3

## Parallel Worlds: Writing a Difficult Letter

Dear Mr. And Mrs. A.,

This first marking period has been filled with many challenging experiences for both the students and me: the teacher in Room four.

Having a set of identical twins possessing extremely creative minds in the same class presents the need for the teacher to adjust and adapt.

Doug is the twin who learns quickly and adapts well to change. Charlie is more pensive and usually requires at least one review in order to master a new concept or skill.

As identical twins in the same class, Charlie and Doug vacillate between wanting to be paired with each other and establishing a separate identity.

And, if the behavior in school reflects life at home, the A. household must be filled with fun as well as frustration.

By combining creative minds, they have devised a system which has made my job to evaluate their academic progress quite confusing and complex.

So, I will be establishing a reward system for the rest of the class by rewarding other members of the class privileges and prizes in exchange for "ratting "on either of the clever twins, each time the twins try to trick me by:

1. changing clothes with each other followed by or along with…

2. hanging seats with each other or vice versa

3. switching papers and/or assignments and/or switching their names on daily classroom assignments and on assessments as well.

Although their little capers can be viewed as amusing, they interfere with my ability to determine who has mastered what skill, and which boy requires additional practice or reinforcement.

I look forward to the further discussion on this topic at our upcoming parent teacher conference.

Jumping up after having been in a deep sleep can be very disorienting. Although my clock indicated that I had overslept, I quickly realized that it was Saturday and could go back to sleep or just relax under my new satiny quilt for a while longer. And thank goodness that the nightmare/dream I had been having was far from my own reality.

The twins in my class in no way resemble the boys who appeared in my dream. Dean and Carl, my real-life twins, are amusing and cooperative. They also demonstrated the same creativity as their older sister Dawn who I had taught the year before.

What fun it has been getting to know these two clever boys!

Dean and Carl make a dynamic combo together and also are very unique individuals.

## Chapter 4

## Mom is a Smuggler

Dear Mrs. O.,

I hope that this letter concerning your son's snack choices will be the last one I have to write.

I must reiterate that I, as the classroom teacher, do not create the guidelines for accepted choices for students in our school to be included on the list sent home to all families of students who attend our school.

This list is published by the State of New Jersey and approved by the state PTA and the State Board of Education. You are welcomed in my classroom at any time to read the in-depth publication which Mrs. H., our nurse, keeps in her file cabinet.

I can assure you, that Hershey chocolate kisses and M&M candies do not meet the qualifications to be included on that official list.

So, Mrs. O., it would be best if you would end the routine of arriving outside our classroom door each morning at the approximate time that our class has our morning snack break, asking to speak to your son S. and administer some doctor prescribed medications.

The cameras in the hallway contain the necessary proof to corroborate the information necessary to have you banned from entering our building.

Please consider this as fair warning. Stuffing S's pockets with M&Ms and Hershey Kisses is NOT acceptable.

PS
Mrs. H., our school nurse, is planning a workshop in the near future entitled "How to Trick Your Child into Eating a Healthier Diet."

Keep on the lookout for the exact time and date I believe it will also be posted in the agenda for the next PTA meeting.

Sincerely,

Ellen Lewis

## Chapter 5

## All Wet

*The following letter was written by two of my students to the new principal, who had just arrived at her new position.*

Dear A.,

Bobby and I would like to apologize for squirting you with our water guns last week. Ms. Lewis told us the next day that you were going to be the new principal of Schoenly School.

We want you to know that we do not usually bring water guns to school. But Dr. Vaz had been playing a kind of game with us. He was showing up several times a week and catching us by surprise with his water gun attacks.

So, Bobby and I thought of a plan.

We thought if Bobby would stand behind the door when it opened at the time Dr Vaz made his usual morning visit, we would squirt him from both sides. We made this plan with Ms. M.'s approval and cooperation.

On every field day, Ms. Lewis gets soaked with water from a little prank that Dr Vaz plays on her, so she was very happy to help us with our plan.

Unfortunately, the day we planned to carry out our plan was the same day you came along with Dr Vaz, while making his morning visits to the schools. We were aiming at him, not you, when the door opened but somehow you got in the way.

Bobby and I are very sorry for getting you wet. At least it was one of the hottest days so far in June, so your clothes probably got dry pretty quick.
Everyone in the class is also sorry for laughing but you really had a weird look on your face after getting squirted with so much water!

We want you to know that you were not our target. So so please accept our apology.

Bobby and I will be moving up to Appleby School for second grade, but we hope you will like being the new principal at Schoenly.

Both of us had fun and learned a lot in kindergarten and first grade, while we were students here.

Your friends,

Bobby and Miles

# Chapter 6

## The Apple Doesn't Fall Far from the Tree

Dear Mrs. L,

M. is benefitting from the extra help he is now receiving from the members of our Basic Skills staff, who are providing him with reinforcement lessons three times each week in both math and reading. Please continue to motivate him to do his best and not feel defeated when he encounters tricky words and gets confused when doing multistep math problems involving addition and subtraction.

I am pleased that you have acknowledged the fact that M. has been demonstrating some inappropriate behaviors since you and his father have separated. It is understandable that children may 'act out' during these times of emotional stress.

But the behaviors which negatively impact other students in the class are unacceptable. Because your house is on the same block as our school, M. can run home quickly and arrive within minutes of dismissal.

However, running to his bedroom, locking the door, and shouting out curse words from his bedroom window targeting some of the girls from our class as they pass your house on their way home, is an unacceptable behavior that must immediately be extinguished.

Since your home is not on school property there is nothing, I can do legally but I am sure you can empathize with the parents of these girls and will do whatever you can to discourage M. from this prank he has initiated.

I appreciate you sharing the fact that M. has learned these words from his father with whom he visits each weekend.

But now that your mother is living with you, which has enabled you to obtain a full-time job, perhaps she will be able to supervise the after-school situation better than your neighbor's teenage daughter had.

However, I am glad that we both agree that the present situation is unacceptable.

Our goal, as always, is to work together to support M.

Sincerely,

Ellen Lewis

**Reply letter.**

Dear Mrs. Lewis,

Let me know if M. starts using those cuss words again with those little girls who are in the class, I want you to know that I called his 'son of a bitch of a father' and threatened to take him to court if don't stop usin' all those damn cuss words around my M.!

Mrs. L.

# Chapter 7

## Antiseptic Student Teacher

One of my last student teachers, a school librarian, appeared at first to be a natural fit. Mrs. E. was a known entity because she was a member of the same church as my principal. And her library experience combined with her knowledge of basic educational concepts hinted at the possibility of my having been dealt a winning hand.

During her first few days Mrs. E. observed the routines as well as the dynamics within my classroom. During that introductory phase she meticulously filled up several legal pads with copious amounts of notes about classroom procedures that would be helpful as she transitioned from observing to teaching.

The note taking exercise transformed into a more specific and detailed dimension, almost frenzied, when Mrs. E. entered the classroom armed with post-it pads of every size and color.

She started to literally shadow me throughout the entire day, standing or sitting within inches of me as I taught one to one, in small groups and whole class/ every word I said was on a post it somewhere in my classroom!

Starting from 8:30 a.m. with "Good morning, boys and girls," to at 3:20 p.m. with "Show me what first graders do when they are waiting for the dismissal bell to ring!"

And then, posting these self-adhering snippets of paper on to the nearest object: a wall, the back of a chair, a piece of furniture, a map, the American flag, a globe, a bookshelf, a tissue box , a stack of paper towels a box of straws ... any object that had been in the closest proximity to where I stood while presenting my lesson.

Afterwards, for the next several days, she repeated this technique. During lunch and recess or when the students were at a special class like music, phys. ed or art, she followed her path of 'post-its' around the classroom reading and reciting the words on these mini papers in the order they were posted as if she were rehearsing and memorizing lines for a play.

Each day, depending on the lessons, I had planned, the forest of 'post-its' grew.

Can you picture what my classroom looked like? Imagine the aftermath of a ticker tape parade meets massive Piñata party!

Even more amazing and amusing was watching Mrs. E. deliver direct and specific orders to the night custodian forbidding him from touching any part of her uncultivated thicket.

One morning, as we were completing week two of this growing spectacle, Mrs. E. announced that her allergies were interfering with her ability to function and began to toss all my classroom items on the list, given to her by her allergist, into two huge plastic tubs, which she had lugged into the building.

By the time she completed her task, all that was left in my room were the books in student desks, curriculum-related texts and assorted classroom library books on the shelves, a few reams of paper, some number-two pencils, a collection of old wooden rulers, and a few tarnished steel scissors.

Having a classroom in the primary grades provides an opportunity to showcase how to integrate the curriculum, translating into the inclusion of creative projects to enhance student growth and understanding. These activities would now be eliminated, along with the tools and materials used to create them.

"Not to worry," Mrs. E. assured me. "I bought a giant roll of butcher block paper."

As she went to look for a custodian to get some help storing the discards from my room, she handed me a list of food products that could aggravate her allergic issues and therefore would no longer be allowed in my classroom This ban could work well for me. I might finally lose that extra ten pounds I have been trying to lose for most of my post-menopausal life.

But whose job would it be to deliver this news to the parents?

After a string of days of me watching and listening, while Mrs. E. waltzed around my classroom picking post-its off walls and furniture and reading my words over and over again, and eyeing the roll of butcher block paper that Mrs. E. had purchased get skinnier each day, as she literally wrapped my classroom room in the allergically acceptable wall covering and feeling each time I walked into my classroom that I was becoming engulfed inside a giant sized UPS package, I desperately needed to determine at what point this ridiculous escapade was going to end.

After allowing for a suitable adjustment period, my pedagogical instinct told me that I needed to get the situation under control. The following morning, I suggested to my principal that she schedule a meeting to deal with and hopefully adjust to the unprecedented interruption and interference with the established classroom routines.

In the end ... if my Wellesley /Harvard educated principal gained anything to add to her repertoire of administrative skills from this wretched situation, it might be found in MY adaptation of a quote from the famed English historian Arnold Toynbee, which as revised would read, "The supreme accomplishment is to MAXIMIZE the line between "WORK" and "PRAY!""

After several weeks of meetings resulting in frustrations and tears, the student teacher withdrew from the program stating that, "The school district refused to comply with the recommendations necessary to meet her needs.

## Chapter 8

## Dancing the Macarena

Dear R.,

You expressed shock in your letter to me protesting the fact that you received a failing grade for your semester in student teaching. I realize that not too many school districts will hire an applicant who has failed this part of the training in which the educational theory is applied and learning goals are met.

However, R., it was your attitude combined with the absence of an acceptable work ethic which were the deciding factors in determining your grade. Initially you appeared to be eager to commit yourself to the complete the necessary work required to create instruction which reflected the need to include a variety of modalities so that all students could succeed.

I recall that on that Monday morning, you entered my classroom and announced that, after having been assigned the weekend task of preparing lessons to be taught during the upcoming school week, that I "must be crazy to expect you to spend your whole weekend wasting so much time figuring out what to teach and how to teach it!"

That moment was punctuated in my memory when you slammed my books back onto my desk with a thud and stomped out of the classroom.

You did do a commendable job persuading even the most reluctant of students to join with other class members in learning the new Latin dance called the Macarena. When teaching the class this dance you demonstrated an intuitive sense of the learning theory similar to that of Madeline Hunter, who is highly respected in the field of education today.

I must also add how thrilled many of the mothers of our students were when their children demonstrated this new dance at home and then taught interested family members all the hand gestures and steps that are part of this popular dance.

And I must admit, even though you chose not to teach any of the lesson plans which were entered in the plan book you were given, they were expertly written.

Unfortunately, you should not have stopped dating your fellow education major from Jersey City University, who had also been assigned to one of the Kindergarten classes in my school, because she informed both her cooperating teacher and the professor in charge of the student teaching program at the University at the semester's end, that she had actually written all of the plans you submitted.

In hindsight, it was not a wise decision, R., to break up with this girl BEFORE taking her to the Senior Weekend Dance hosted by her Campus Sorority.

And finally, R., your parting words for me did not sound like words that reflected a future of a promising educator.

"Goodbye, Miz Lewis," you said, with a huge smirk on your face. "My cousin just got me a job working on a sanitation truck in Jersey City."

"My starting salary, you might care to know, will be more than you are making after almost twenty years in the classroom!"

Hmmm.

Do your parting words for me on your last day in my classroom, your very last chance to inspire me with even an iota of educationally related enthusiasm, suggest that you would be shocked to receive a grade in student teaching from me that wasn't an "F" ?

Good luck to you.

From,

Ellen Lewis

## Chapter 9

## Shenanigans

Here are some of my scattered memories:

1. How embarrassed I was for my first student teacher when he realized that he could not pass the first-grade spelling test he was assigned to administer at the end of the week.

2. Realizing my good fortune in having incredible bladder control, unlike some of my fellow teachers who I would often see racing around the corner and down the hallway past my classroom heading for the teachers' restroom.

3. Our annual Field Day which always officially began with an amusing prank during the years when Tony V. was our principal. I would not have been surprised to learn that Tony devised this plan when reminiscing about college fraternity initiations.

On the day which had been designated as "Field Day," F., the custodian, would arrive at school early in order to complete his routine work before dragging a trash barrel and a hose, which he connected to the school's water system onto the roof.

Tony V., who monitored the teachers parking lot would wave a flag signaling my arrival to T. By the time I reached the front door the custodian had already placed the trash barrel now filled to the top with water directly above the main entrance to the school. So, all he had to do was tip the barrel and aim its contents right down on my head until my entire body was thoroughly soaked!

Within minutes I was surrounded with the laughs and cheers from those who enjoyed arriving early to witness the "OFFICIAL" beginning of Field Day.

    4. My first field trip. It was 1973 and Nell Burgeson and I chose to take our first graders on a journey to the New York Botanical Gardens. She and I enlisted all the chaperones to follow our lead and keep our first graders within our eyesight at all times.

Upon surveying the group near the conclusion of the visit, I suddenly realized that one of my parent chaperones was missing! The thought of returning to school missing a mother was unthinkable.

After reviewing the afternoon's events Nell and I surmised that while the students were immersed in a project with the staff at the Gardens, Mrs. S., one of my mothers, had wandered away from the group unnoticed.

Just like Hansel and Gretel, she had most likely taken a few too many twists and turns while exploring the acres of horticultural displays.

Thank goodness for the surveillance cameras and two groundskeepers, who found her at the far end of the park trying but failing to retrace her steps.

> 5. The next year we chose the Philadelphia Zoo as our destination. I volunteered to be the teacher in charge of all planning. After all, I thought to myself, I had planned a trip to Europe the summer following college graduation. If I could do that successfully, a trip to Philly would be a cinch!!

I spent hours creating activities and assignments to be completed by the students while investigating and observing animal life. However, when determining the cost of the trip per child, I had only taken the transportation costs into consideration.

On the morning of the trip, I proudly gave the funds I had collected to the school secretary to deposit in the school account so she could pay the bus company.

But... It was not until the bus entered the parking area of the zoo that I realized I had never collected money for admission. Thank heavens I had just paid off my credit card, because even with the discount for school groups, the cost for the two first grade classes plus chaperones were almost one-hundred dollars.

I was more than thankful to the warm-hearted supportive parents who accompanied the class to the zoo! Because within a week after going to Philadelphia, these mothers collected the admission fees from all the parents whose children had been on the trip in order to reimburse me.

And they accomplished this fete without my principal, a gentleman who had zero tolerance for errors, especially for those of us who were the newest crop of fledglings, ever finding out!

The realization that I was in a dicey predicament.

6. When, as a first-year teacher, having made plans with a group of friends to meet at a local venue one Friday night, I was lucky to get one of the coveted seats at the bar. Within a minute or two I was approached by a gentleman who I vaguely recognized.

It took me a few minutes to make the connection, but… I got "goose bumps" upon realizing that his guy who was putting the moves on me was the father of one of my first graders!

It was obvious that he knew who I was and that despite the awkward situation he continued his pursuit.

"I was not aware that you and A's mom were not together," I said.

His response left me dumbfounded!

(This was despite knowing that the concept of "open marriage" was beginning to take root amidst the 'free thinkers' who considered themselves as open minded and uninhibited during the early 1970's.)

"We have an understanding!" he matter-of-factly announced.

"R.'s mother believes, as I do, that some of us require multiple partners to satisfy our needs. And I have no doubt that she would wholeheartedly approve of you as my selection."

"Well, I'm not so sure my husband would feel the same way," I added while walking away.

I was not surprised when the following week R's dad was a "No Show" for the parent teacher conference which had been scheduled weeks earlier. A's mom apologized profusely when informing me that her husband had been called out of town to attend an unexpected business meeting!

# Part II

# There's Only so Much a Teacher Can Do

## Chapter 10

## There is Only So Much a Teacher Can Do

Somehow the children who appeared to be the most emotionally in need were assigned to my class. S. was one of those students a teacher never forgets. His situation was one of the most heartbreaking I can recall from all my years in the classroom.

One of the neediest students during the span of my career was S. He bore the scars of battle but there was always a smile on his face. Dad was in jail. Mom and a sibling had both been victims of dad's violent nature. The sibling, a ten-year-old sister, had been placed into a state mental institution by the division of family services to heal the physical and emotional wounds resulting from her abusive father.

During the year S. spent in my class he began the process of healing his wounds, which allowed him to grow academically and psychologically, and to enjoy being the sweet little boy who had been hiding behind the aggressive mask he had created in his efforts to survive. It was a joy to observe him blossom and thrive.

The following year I checked in each week with my friend and colleague, the second-grade teacher with whom I had entrusted S. to monitor his progress. We were both thrilled at how much he continued to thrive.

At the end of his year in second grade S's sister had healed enough to be released from the hospital and returned home to be followed up with outpatient treatment. Mom had gotten a job and both children continued to progress until A. was in third grade and ...... the court granted S's father early parole.

Within weeks after getting out of prison, S.'s father was back home and after a matter of months I heard that S. had begun to regress. Since I did not know S's third grade teacher, it was more difficult to be apprised of the events taking place in S's life until I received a message from our school nurse.

S. had been found unconscious on the floor of the basement of his house, having failed in an attempt to hang himself. His sister had been placed back into the institution and mom had fallen into a catatonic state.

# Chapter 11

# Coincidences

Throughout my years as a classroom teacher, there were times when I served as the union rep for my building. It was not unusual for non-tenured teachers to ask for my assistance to help in dealing with issues related to teaching contracts.

I was not surprised when one of the teachers, Mrs. L., who was up for tenure, asked me for advice. She had not been given a contract for the following school year, which when signed would have assured her of attaining that secure tenured position.

I knew little about her, other than she had been a lawyer in her previous career but decided to become a teacher after having her children.

I never observed anything unusual about her and was never in her classroom while students were present. We didn't share the same lunch period and I had little need for interaction beyond the formalities of greetings.

After several discussions about her contract, I suggested that she use her legal expertise to find some small detail to hold the board of education accountable for screwing up in some way, which would enable her to instantly make their case moot. This she did, and she became a member of the tenured staff.

Basically, I had not given much thought to this teacher for years, until I was assigned to work in a local school two years ago in my part-time job for the state. This job provides reinforcement for students in non-public schools based on standardized test scores.

During the school year 2021-2022, while working for the Commission, I had been assigned to work with a young girl at the junior high level, who was struggling to succeed because of a severe learning handicap. As we became more comfortable with each other over the school year, she began to share things about her family with me.

One day she was talking about her younger brother. I was surprised to discover that although she had been enrolled at this religious school, her younger brother attended a public school in the town where they lived.

Coincidentally, the school her brother was attending was the school in which I had taught for over three decades.

Eventually over the next weeks, I built up the courage to ask why her brother was in a public school while she was being sent to a religious academy. (This seemed unusual in my experience. Immigrant families like A.'s usually made one choice for their children's education: either public school OR a school affiliated and sponsored by their religious affiliation.)

Upon hearing my question, A. became extremely agitated and asked to be excused. As I was walking to my next class, I noticed her standing in front of the girl's restroom wiping several tears away from her eyes.

The next time when I met with her for our weekly session, she apologized for her abrupt departure from class, and offered a heartbreaking story that answered more questions than I would ever need to ask.

"You see, Miss Ellen," she said, "I attended kindergarten in the public school, the one where you used to teach. Right after starting kindergarten, it became apparent that I had many learning issues. My parents could not help because as immigrants they were just learning the language."

"Who was your teacher?" I asked even though I thought I already knew the answer.

With tears streaming down her face A. whispered, "Mrs. L."

"I cried every day in her class," she said. "I was struggling to try to learn the language but also had a learning disability. Every time I cried, Mrs. L. would come to my table and pull off my hijab and pull my hair."

"When she really got angry, she would pull me off my chair and drag my body along the floor."

"All the students were afraid of her and even more afraid to tell."

"She never got caught."

Finally, I asked A. my last question.

"Did you tell your parents?"

"I did," she explained.

"But," she added, "They could barely speak English themselves. They had temporary visas. They were afraid."

"Then a friend of my parents suggested that I might be more welcomed here at Dural Agwam."

Although I was not reassigned to her school for the next school year, I often think about A. and how fortunate she was to have found a welcoming and supportive academic environment, and how ashamed I feel to have been associated with someone who allegedly treated an innocent child with such disdain.

One of my ex-colleagues recently invited me to join her for lunch with Mrs. L.

I expressed my regrets, and since they are friends, I am still trying to explain why that lunch date will never happen.

If I should ever have the opportunity to be in the presence of Mrs. L. and if I have no indications that there is any problem with the truth of what A shared with me, I might consider posing one question to my ex-colleague.

"How can anyone explain and justify the treatment that was given to a young innocent child while she was in your class?"

## Chapter 12

## Abused and Acting Out

Dear Mr. X.,

I appreciate that you were able to rearrange your schedule to speak with Mrs. S., our principal, and me on the speaker phone this afternoon.

I am sorry that we disrupted your meeting and that it caused some problems with your business associates who arrived from Russia this morning to discuss the crisis occurring in your "multi-million dollar" business.

But Mrs. S. and I are extremely concerned about your son, O. He is finding it increasingly difficult to control his anger when frustrating circumstances arise. His violent actions cannot be tolerated in our school!

It has been difficult for O. to adjust to your separation from his mother especially on the nights she works at the new Russian night club you have recently opened in Staten Island.

Unfortunately, the caretaker you hired for O. speaks no English and I am not sure that he monitors O.'s activities as much as he should. O. has also shared some stories about a few questionable people who often stop by the apartment and who are providing unsuitable influence on such a young boy.

O. has also been confiding in our school nurse this week about the bruising on his back which he told her was a result of beatings he received over the weekend from his grandfather, who he visited on Staten Island.

If we are not able to arrange a meeting in the next few days, Mrs. S. and I will have no choice but to notify the Division of Family Services and refer O. to the Child Welfare Bureau.

It is important that meet within the next few days to discuss these disturbing issues.

Sincerely,

Ellen Lewis

## Chapter 13

## Cochlear Crisis

Dear Dr. Q.,

I am writing this letter in response to your reaction to the note my doctor sent to you regarding my return to work.

As you know, in December I contracted a stubborn stomach virus which resulted in uncontrolled vomiting for three days. My family doctor refused to prescribe the suppository form of the medication, nor would she permit me in the office to get an injection.

Finally, after three days of delivering meds that would only be vomited before they could become effective, my local pharmacist, Steve L., broke with protocol and delivered the appropriate form of the meds needed. By the end of the day the vomiting ceased. Unfortunately, by this time I had lost my equilibrium.

The next morning, I called my ENT doctor in New York. He made the necessary arrangements for me to meet him at Lenox Hill Hospital, where he performed emergency surgery.

I was fortunate to be a patient of Dr Ronald H., a well-respected and extremely talented doctor who performed the operation. He did the best he could but was unable to save the cochlea in my right ear, which had been totally shattered. Besides explaining to me that I had permanently lost 80% of the hearing in my right ear, Dr. H. informed me that due to the delicacy of the surgery I would be experiencing a loss of equilibrium until what was left of the inner ear could heal.

After about three weeks at home, Dr H. determined that I could return to school but with limitations. He insisted that my work hours be limited to only those when my students were present. That meant no early arrivals on my part and leaving the building at dismissal. He made it clear that there be no exceptions. This meant that I would be unable to attend faculty meetings until further notice.

I was thrilled to be going back to work!

And Dr. Q., I thought you would be pleased as well, until I watched as you tore up the letter after reading Dr. H.'s medical recommendations.

As you threw out these shreds in the trash you exclaimed, "No Fancy Doctor from New York City is going to tell me how to run my school!"

I cannot begin to explain my anger and disappointment at your reaction! It does not represent the kind of leadership qualities I might have expected from a principal and fellow educator.

With regrets,

Ellen Lewis

## Update and Addendum

At the next post-op visit with Dr H. weeks after Dr Q.'s outburst, I shared the reaction to his instructions with him. The anger I heard in his voice surpassed whatever I could have ever imagined!

"I am a well-respected member of the medical community!" he said. "I have written letters with my recommendations to the Presidents and CEOs of major corporations as well as heads of state. Never in my wildest dreams could I imagine my guidelines being discarded in such a disrespectful manner.

"If you decide to take legal action against this, *BITCH,* I want to be the first one on the witness stand!"

I returned to school but continued my battle with Dr Q. concerning the criteria that Dr H. had established to help avoid post-surgical complications.

I called my teachers association representative, asking to schedule a meeting with the principal to discuss the matter.

When the day of the meeting arrived, I was surprised that it was Mrs. T., the local district's NJEA president, who appeared. After Dr Q. restated her expectations for me as far as resuming work was concerned, Mrs. T. suggested she and the principal continue the meeting in the principal's office.

After about fifteen minutes Mrs. T. asked me to join them, at which time she announced that I was to abide by my principal's requests and ignore my doctor's orders.

I felt humiliated, discouraged, and exhausted.

That evening I called Mrs. T. at home and asked her to explain her actions. Her response was one I could never have anticipated .

"I am a United States citizen," she began, "but I am also an Arab. When I learned that you were a Jew, I realized I had only one choice in this matter. I hate Jews and I would never to anything to help one of you!"

## Chapter 14

## Signing Out

Dear Mrs. C.,

I understand that the beginning of this school year has been a difficult one academically for D. However, I can assure you that I do not dislike D., who is a lovely soft-spoken boy.

D. has been struggling to master the skills needed to become a more independent reader. Reading is a developmental process and as I stated at our last meeting, just like young children do not all learn to walk and talk on the same day, children differ in the amount of time necessary to develop the skills needed to master the written word.

Miss A., our principal, who attended last night's Board of Education meeting, was surprised to hear you publicly accuse me of not making any effort to teach D. to read. According to your statement, I only teach my favorite students how to read. Do you have a list of these favorite students and the assessments that reflect their progress?

This morning, I received an interesting call from one of the board members. This board member reported to me that you spoke with him privately and told him that D.

was reading at home and that he could read excerpts from the encyclopedia as well as books that your daughter was reading in the sixth grade.

However, that statement contradicts your previous accusation that D. could not read! So, I need clarification. Is the problem that D. cannot read or is it that he can read, but only at home?

This board member also shared a comment that you made to him after you gave the matter additional thought. You explained that D. was an extremely sensitive boy and that I was a very demanding teacher and because of the harsh treatment I meted out, he was too scared to read in my presence! That statement has no validity, and I would ask you to substantiate that assertion with any applicable evidence.

Due to the contradictory nature of your statements, both this board member and I remain confused and wary of your accusations. However, if you share a video tape or cassette tape of D. reading at home, it will help me formulate a more accurate assessment of his reading progress.

I am hoping that these misunderstandings can be resolved in a more professional manner in the future rather than you resorting to publicly announcing your theories as facts.

Yours truly,

Ellen Lewis

## Chapter 15

## Sadly True, Alice's Story

Dear Ms. F.,

I do not take your threats to my life lightly. But neither do I take lightly my job as an educator and guardian for the safety of the young children with whom I spend seven hours of each day teaching.

When a child falls asleep in my classroom, that usually is an indication of trouble somewhere. What Alice disclosed to our school nurse this week suggested that the issues in your home situation need immediate intervention, despite your denials.

No innocent first grader should be told when asking who her father is, "HE WAS JUST SOME GUY WHO I picked up one night in Florida!"

No little girl should spend her time at home entertaining her mother's clients, as they funnel in and out of her mother's bedroom.

No six-year-old should be the appointed messenger and get sent to the local liquor store to replenish her mother's liquor closet at 9 o'clock at night, by walking down a poorly lit two-lane country road, to get mommy's friends some refills.

And no child who wakes up in a stupor at midnight after collapsing on her bedroom floor should have to look out the window to see her mother drive away to visit Auntie Mary.

And no young child should be left alone to take care of the empty bottles and cans and as well as being responsible for straightening the apartment before mommy gets home with breakfast in the morning.

If it wasn't me bringing this horrific circumstance to the attention of the authorities it would be someone else.

I appreciate your alerting me to the fact that you followed me home and know where I live. But the police have been to your home and spoken to your neighbors.

And they have a record of the threats you have made to my life.

Need I say more?

Sincerely,

Ellen Lewis

# Chapter 16

## Mrs. H.'s Protest

Dear Mrs. H.,

I have just attended a meeting with Dr. V., our Superintendent of Schools, and Mrs. D., our principal, as well as our reading consultant, concerning the appropriate and most beneficial placement for your son J. in reading instruction. It is important to all concerned that J. receives the literacy instruction that best meets his needs. Our goal is to help him build a solid foundation in language arts.

It was disturbing to learn that at last night's Board of Education's monthly meeting that you announced to all who attended that you, as J.'s mother, have become convinced that my decision to reassign John to a less challenging reading group, indicated my ineptness as his teacher.

Therefore, you are demanding to have access to my weekly lesson plans so that you can determine whether or not the objectives and activities that I prepare meet with your approval and appropriately address your son's aptitude. And that you as the parent, not Mrs. D. the principal, will either approve or disapprove of these weekly instructional plans.

My decision to reassign J. to the "middle reading group" and not the group of students who are working at a more accelerated pace, was based upon J.'s daily performance as well as his scores on the unit assessment which was created by the textbook publishers. The students who remained in the reading group in which he had been working had mastered the skills necessary to move on to assignments of a more advanced academic level. J.'s test results reflected the need for further practice to achieve mastery before moving on.

I have concerns about your motivation in making your public announcement last evening. I know that you were extremely disturbed when I made the decision about J. being assigned to a different reading group, but the results of the testing done by the reading specialist and reported at today's meeting mirrored my findings and reinforced my actions.

So, if the goal of your public outburst was to anger and humiliate me, you have succeeded. But can you imagine what might occur if you chose to abstain from crude announcements and finger pointing and instead became part of a united team, with the goal of helping J. to succeed?

Sincerely,

Ellen Lewis

## Outcome

I learned years later that I was the only teacher in this student's history in the primary grades who did not succumb to the pressure from this overly pushy parent. I eventually questioned the teachers who caved to her demands. Their responses were all similar: "Why fight the battle?" " Who needs the aggravation?" and "Why should I make myself sick because of her?"

This mother did her best to destroy whatever part of my reputation she could. Many parents, after talking with her, refused to allow their children to be assigned to my class. From what I understand, my name was included in a list that circulated among parents listing the names of the worst teachers in the district. I was told by someone many years later, after the family had moved, that Mrs. H. complained that none of the teachers in the new town recognized her son's true intelligence.

The last I heard of Mrs. H. was that she thought that it was disgraceful that none of the colleges which she had selected for her son to attend granted him admission.

Fortunately for me, my supporters far outweighed Mrs. H's brigade of naysayers.

## Chapter 17

## Teacher Robs Student

Dear Mrs. V.,

I am writing this letter in response to the incriminating statement you made to Mr. C., our principal, during the conference call we shared this afternoon.

It is appalling that you would accuse me of being a thief and a liar.

I did not rummage through my students' desks.

I did not take any envelopes from any desks.

I did not rip up any envelopes and stuff them into the trashcan in the boy's bathroom.

And I did not place over $5 in coins and dollar bills into your son, M's desk.

Where did you get these ideas? How could you possibly think that I could or would possibly do something so ridiculously senseless?

During the phone call this afternoon, Mr. C. explained to you that he had received several calls from parents of children in our class expressing concern about lunch money that each of these children had been given to purchase lunch, milk, or juice. Most children put those envelopes inside their desks or kept them in their lockers which are inside the classroom. However, when lunchtime arrived the money and envelopes had disappeared.

According to the staff who serves lunch in our school our class accrues more "charge slips for lunch than any other class in the school."

So, Mr. C. and I resolved to solve this mystery. Then today, without even my knowledge, Mr. C. abruptly interrupted our class activities just after lunch this afternoon. Two children had charged lunch that day because they could not locate the envelope with their lunch money. After doing this unannounced search of the desks and lockers in our classroom, Principal C. called each child into his office for a chat in hopes of gaining some information pertaining to the mystery.

When it was M's turn to speak with Mr. C., M. was asked to explain the fact that he had $5.26 in dollar bills and coins inside his desk. M. offered no response.

After M. returned to the classroom Mr. C. contacted you about the issue in hopes that you might provide further important information. Most first graders do not carry money to school with them unless there is a specific purpose, i.e., lunch money, a book fair, or a PTA fundraiser for example.

M. did tell Mr. C. that he rarely if ever bought either lunch, or ice cream or milk or juice at school because he preferred to eat what his mother made for him.

As Mr. C. explained and emphasized during our phone conversation, "No allegations have been made and no one has been accused of anything," which makes me wonder why you have been so quick to accuse me in the conversation today of taking the money and then hiding it in M's desk.

And then, coincidently, on my way home from school today I stopped at the supermarket. As always, Shop Rite was extremely busy. And while waiting in line to check out, the woman ahead of me turned around and in a very "loud whisper," announced the latest gossip.

"Did you hear what happened today at one of the elementary schools?"

"Can you imagine this?"

"One of the teachers stole money from her students' desks and lockers, money that was intended for them to buy lunch……."

"And then after stealing the money, this teacher "planted it" inside the desk of an innocent little boy and blamed it all on him!"

"Everyone is talking about it and trying to find out what the kids know about this dreadful behavior!"

No words, can adequately define my state of mind after hearing this obviously well-traveled story loaded with false allegations.

Was this effort to spread malicious gossip really necessary Mrs. V.?

And just what kind of example do you think you are establishing for your son by using tactics like this?

Sincerely,

Ellen Lewis

# Part III

# Teaching is the Greatest Act of Optimism

## Chapter 18

## Advice for a Student Teacher

Dear Mrs. Gerard,

I am preparing the final paperwork to send to the university along with your grade for the student teaching experience. You have many qualities that make you an excellent candidate for becoming a certified teacher in the state of New Jersey.

1) You are motivated and you are receptive to all kinds of suggestions to grow as a classroom teacher.

2) You have an excellent work ethic and are attentive when I model lessons for you and suggest sources that you can investigate in the most accepted theories of transitioning from theory into instruction.

3) The students and parents sense your enthusiasm and are responsive to your presence in our classroom and some parents have spoken with Dr K. about how pleased they are with the good job you are doing.

4) I have never seen you without a smile. Even when you are upset the smile on your face hides any anguish that you are feeling.

There are, however, issues that Mr. C., our principal, asked me to discuss with you during the semester.

Cell phone usage

There are limits to cell phone usage for all teachers on the staff. Most teachers in the building either shut off their phone or mute the ringer. Unfortunately, Mr. C. and I both have had to speak with you several times concerning this issue.

Mr. C.'s decision followed a mandate from central office. Both Dr K. and Mr. C. were aware that your husband was serving in another country but there had to have been better times and places to receive such calls.

2) Appearance

Mr. C. has questioned some of your clothing choices that have been inappropriate for the classroom, including midriff tops with hip hugger pants. Some of your sweaters and tee shirts revealed your undergarments while other low cut very tight sweaters and tee shirts you chose to wear although popular were not suited for a teaching professional.

3) Fundamentals of lesson preparation

And finally, Mr. C. and I are still quite puzzled about the day Dr. K., our Superintendent of Schools, visited the classroom to observe you teach a lesson.

You and I had discussed how beneficial having a letter of recommendation from someone as well respected as Dr. K. would be when seeking a teaching position. He specifically rearranged his schedule to be available for this observation because he had heard so many positive comments about you from parents.

So, we worked together and produced a lesson which contained all the right pedagogical elements and one that I was sure Dr. K. would appreciate.

But the lesson you presented was not the one we worked on together and had none of those elements. And what made matters worse was the fact that the topic of the lesson was synonyms, but your lesson was about describing words and you repeatedly referred to the adjectives in your lesson as synonyms.

Ten minutes into the lesson Dr. K. excused himself politely and exited the classroom and the school. Mr. C. took his lead from Dr. K. and shaking his head pointed in my direction mouthing the words before his departure…"My office 3 o'clock!"

You were lucky, Mrs. Gerard, that we had carefully prepared the students about appropriate behaviors when important visitors were in the room, because they realized that the objective of your lesson was to be to identify and use synonyms. But the lesson you presented was about describing words (and adjectives) and you continuously referred to them as synonyms. This class is a very well-behaved group of children and know the kinds of behavior that is expected of them when important visitors are in the classroom.

They displayed appropriate and respectful behavior which not all classes might do in similar circumstances. I am so glad that I promised them the reward of having their math test cancelled that afternoon and going out to the playground if their behavior was impeccable.

Later when I asked you what made you change the lesson we had worked on, your answer was understandable but unwise.

"Well," you explained. "Last night after dinner, I demonstrated two lessons for my mother, one which I had prepared a day or two ago and the one on which we practiced after school."

"Both my mother and I agreed that my lesson was better because it was more original and reflected more of my personality."

Mrs. Gerard, that choice may prove to limit your opportunities in the future.

Wishing you well.

Yours truly,

Ellen Lewis

## Chapter 19
## A Leader Emerges

To Christopher and his family,

Many times, when a teacher sends a letter home, the purpose is to inform the family of something unpleasant.

Today I send this letter commending Christopher for exemplifying what kindness and compassion really are about.

Many times, when a child transfers to a new school there is a period of adjustment to become accepted. This year, we have a student who is new to our class, new to our school, new to our town and new to our country.

Christopher has reached out to our new classmate with an offering of friendship modeling the way for everyone in the class to follow suit. From the first day of school Christopher viewed Jorge as a welcomed member to our class. Jorge may look tough because of his size but Christopher saw him more as a "gentle giant."

During recess today, when some students from other classes chose to taunt Jorge on the playground, Christopher, who is among the shortest students in the first grade, chose to rally his classmates in order to protect J. and instead of escalating a potentially volatile situation, Christopher being Christopher, intervened on behalf of Jorge and then notified the playground aides.

Those of us who know Christopher consider ourselves to be privileged!

With great admiration,

Mrs. Lewis

## Epilogue
**2023**

At the end of the past summer, I received a message on Facebook from Christopher's mom telling me that he would be starting his first teaching job as a physical education teacher and coach, in one of the schools in my old school district. That news put a smile on my face that lasted for several days.

## Chapter 20

## Script for Back-to-School Night

Welcome parents! Thank you all for coming to the yearly event of Back to School Night. These meet and greet evenings usually take place after the first week or two of school while all students are adjusting to new routines, new classmates, and a new environment physically and academically.

For one of their first assignments, I asked the members of our class to create a self-portrait . The lesson began with me sharing some portraits that were painted by some famous artists. I revealed to the class which of the portraits was my favorite and then modeled the process of creating my own self-portrait by utilizing some of the artist's style.

The second part of the assignment consisted of working together in small groups to compile a list of words people may use when describing themselves.

After the class joined together to create a completed list, I assigned them to write two or more complete sentences, not fragments, to describe themselves. I asked that they not write their names on the completed papers. They were so excited to find out that at 'Back to School Night' each parent would be assigned the challenge of determining which picture and description was created by his or her child.

I enjoy creating lessons in which parents and students are involved. This assignment illustrates how drawing and writing a sentence can be a dynamic experience.

Congratulations to all who participated in the challenge!

Thanks to all of you who are joining me tonight to learn about the journey ahead for your first graders.

## MY Goals and Objectives (and the Means of Accomplishing Them)

1.) Create activities that include partner work and small group work, as well as independent assignments.

2.) NOT teach subject areas in isolation. Instead, I try to incorporate more than one discipline when planning my lessons. So, a reading lesson might have a bit of geography and math infused into the assignment. Research shows that this kind of instruction leads to long term learning.

3) Agree with and follow the lead of theorists like John Dewey, who suggest that students learn best by doing. So, in this class students will be up and about doing as many things as possible that I can create, to make the learning experiences more meaningful and memorable.

4) Recognize and respect the distinct individuals who are members of this class. To encourage each class member to take responsibility for his or her actions and words.

5) Share a few of my personal interests. The activity with which we started this evening represents my desire to share my love of art. Each month I will introduce the class to one of my favorite artists and provide activities to help students become familiar with both the particular genre and guide them in discovering identify characteristics of the work of that particular artist. My choice of artists to introduce the class to is usually related to the particular part of the curriculum on which we are focused.

As an aside, I would like to share with you a memorable moment which was relayed to me by a parent. She told me that she and her son were walking through the mall one day when they stopped to look at a picture that was displayed in a store window. He turned to her and asked, "Mom does this picture remind you more of a Van Gogh or a Monet?" Mom said she was astounded by the question but listened intently as her son described the style of both well-known artists. Our conversation ended with her expressing her gratitude for the bit of enrichment I provided for her first-grade son.

In conclusion, as we embark on this year's journey with a classroom filled with eager curious minds, my mantra continues to emphasize that learning can and should be fun.

It is also important to acknowledge and emphasize that what your child learns this year forms the foundation for all future learning.

These beliefs stated above serve as my guide as I plan the activities and lessons which hopefully will make first grade a successful and exceptional year.

## Chapter 21

## Circle of Life

Dear Tom,

Has it been that many years since the soft-spoken boy with the deep brown eyes and the shiny brown hair was sitting here in my classroom eager to begin his first full day in school as a first-grade student? After so many years of memories of:

--a dance with me, your old first grade teacher at your senior prom, and how we both found it hilarious that because my gown was backless, you struggled finding a place for your hand that was supposed to be on my back as you guided me onto the dance floor.

--you babysitting my son when I was thrust into the role of single motherhood...

--you obeying your mother who insisted that you mow my lawn, which was a bitch to mow because the back yard was the top of a very steep hill...

--me learning of your graduation from college and then getting your law degree, and then moving back to your hometown with your family and being elected as mayor ...

--Memories of the past and learning about the most recent events have all brought such joy to your old first grade teacher.

And now I have been given the privilege of having your oldest child in my first-grade class of 2005/2006!

What an amazing experience to be welcoming your oldest son Collin, as a member of my class in much the same way I greeted you decades ago.

This must be that circle of life referred to in poems and songs.

But for me it is more about the kind of family made of friendship and memories. It is an honor to be extending this journey of joy to the next generation.

Thank you for entrusting your son to me as we enter the world of nurturing and ensuring that his foundation is strong enough to support him along his journey.

With joy,

Ellen Lewis

## Chapter 22

### Don't let Toxic Leaders Get You Down.

I include this last letter because sometimes, to our dismay, there are enemies in our midst. Sadly, I encountered colleagues that were not well-meaning or supportive of teachers. Yet, I found it very powerful, and yes, even optimistic, to address many of them when I discovered their toxic behavior.

If you wonder why I include this real-life account in this book, so dear to me, with a story of such racism, I can explain it well. We will always face parents or colleagues that are abusive. But as educators, we have the tools to work around them, to change things, and to speak out.

As far as I know, there is no cure for optimism - and that's the beauty of being a teacher!

Dear Dr. M.,

I was puzzled as well as alarmed by your written denial that I may not use the classification of "religious observance" as the reason I was requesting to be excused for three days of teaching.

I am aware that the guidelines regarding student absences state that if a student does not attend school because he or she is observing a religious holiday, that absence is excused.

Therefore, I assumed that the same would apply to me as a teacher. So, I was surprised to receive your letter denying my application to classify the three upcoming Jewish High Holy Days as days of religious observance. That is the reason why I stopped by your office after classes were dismissed yesterday thinking there must have been a misunderstanding.

I was saddened to discover that I had not misunderstood your directive.

In the Jewish religion there are two significant holy days. One lasts for two days while the other is observed over a twenty-four-hour period.

According to the school calendar, our school district, unlike most public schools in Middlesex County, will be open on all those days.

Your response was shocking when I questioned your decision. You explained that I, unlike the students, would not be granted those days for my religious observance as excused absences. Your words made it quite clear when you stated, "If it is so important to observe these two holidays, Ellen, you should use your three personal days."

My wide-eyed response reflected my amazement and disbelief.

Your statement implied that because I was Jewish and chose to participate in prayer services during these holiest of days, I would have to use my personal days. To me this was an example of blatant religious discrimination!

I interpreted the meaning of your statement to mean that because I chose to observe my religion, which is a right bestowed upon me by the laws of the United States, I would not have the three personal days in case of an emergency. If I were not of the Jewish faith, I would have those days available should any emergency arise.

While in a state of disbelief I asked you to repeat your directive to be sure I heard your words correctly.

I was astounded by what you said next!

"Wake up, Ellen!" you began. "You teach in a Christian town, and you live in a Christian world! It's time for you to accept who you are and the reality of the world in which you live!!"

How does one digest the statements that had just been made in the year 1996?

Yours,

Ellen Lewis

## Chapter 23

## The Second Shift

One sign of a school filled with pride can be reflected by how well the building is maintained by its custodial staff.

As a teacher who spent long hours well beyond what was stated in the contract, I had the opportunity to work alongside the night crew who were indeed splendid examples of workers with that kind of pride. I considered them my friends.

Jim Rubianos was a veteran of the school system .

After each payday Jim dutifully collected $2 to purchase lottery tickets from each member of a small group of employees who hoped to parlay a few dollars into a windfall of cash. Unfortunately, when it was time for Jim to retire, our best winnings had never amounted to more than enough cash to pay for the pool's next ticket purchase. Our little group never gave up hoping that the next ticket would be the big win. We developed an unspoken connection which was a reward of its own, bonded by our mutual daydreams.

When Jim retired, Leslie was transferred from the high school to take his place. Leslie and I had a little routine. Every day at about 4:30 in the afternoon he would "put up the water for coffee" in the faculty lounge and we would enjoy our daily chat in my classroom.

The chat usually began with whether he or I would retire first, and how much easier it would be if we both had a big bank account to take care of our financial worries.

Leslie was a bachelor and had limited family contact, except for a half sister who he occasionally saw. He had a speech impediment which unfortunately caused him to be reticent to speak to people.

Leslie, thankfully felt comfortable in my presence and had three topics he loved discussing:

1) The king of rock and roll, Elvis Presley
2) His favorite foods
3) Armageddon

Leslie's persona was one of naive kindness that guided both his thoughts and actions.

Ironically, we both left the school district the same year. My unplanned retirement was initiated by a promise I had made to my mother on her death bed.

In Leslie's case, an unplanned and unannounced absence for two days alarmed the school administration and since he had not responded to any efforts to contact him, the police were sent to his apartment.

They found him peacefully lying on his couch. On the coffee table next to him was his favorite Elvis CD and a jar of Skippy Peanut Butter.

It was a privilege for me to have been asked to speak at his memorial service.

# Chapter 24

# Challenging Days Ahead

What is taught in classrooms throughout the United States is based on a specific set of state standards determined by each individual state's department of education. These guides are based on, among other things, the premise of respect for the diverse cultures within each state.

While chatting last June in the elevator with a young teacher who lived in my apartment building as the school term was ending, she confessed that she was not sure she would be able to stay in the field of education for as long as I had.

"The pressures are becoming too great," she began. "This year, for example, there was a group of parents who were opposed to having students of various cultures talk about cultural traditions that they shared with their families at home. Nothing religious had been presented. All conversations were based on discussion of family, food, music and ethnic customs.

"But a group of parents grew angry because they did not think that this kind of information should be part of the school day, despite the fact that it reflected the curriculum based on the standards established by the Department of Education.

"The parents who have been causing the ruckus represent mainstream cooperative parents, not any kind of extremists," continued my young neighbor. "However, they believe that they have the right to determine what is being taught in their children's classroom.

"And the latest rumor, which has not yet been documented is that, despite the fact that Holocaust Studies are required by the state of New Jersey to be taught in the fifth, sixth, seventh, and eighth grades, the principal of my school has begun to collect the material provided by the State Department of Education on this topic and has been telling teachers that we will no longer be responsible for teaching this part of the social studies curriculum.

"I have surmised that since I am the only Jewish teacher in the sixth grade that my principal has not been too eager to share her decision with me."

With that, my young neighbor announced as she exited the elevator with smile, saying, "This is just the "tip of the iceberg."

# Resource Page

**National Education Association (NEA)**
https://www.nea.org/

**Department of Education**
https://www.ed.gov/

**Association for Supervision and Curriculum Development (ASCD)**
https://www.ascd.org/

**Association of American Educators**
https://www.aaeteachers.org/

**Association for Middle Level Education (AMLE)**
https://www.amle.org/

**National Association for Gifted Children (NAGC)**
https://nagc.org/

# Acknowledgements

Above and beyond my Dedication page, there are many people who I must thank.

To the Superintendent whose decision to interpret the idea of religious freedom reflected so poorly upon who he was as a leader and citizen: My religion has taught me that the wisest of us gain strength from our defeats and become wiser by our experiences.

Thank you to Tony Vaz, who was incredible leader as a Superintendent of Schools, and always was a hands-on leader. My son was asthmatic. One time, when he was young, his school nurse called me with an emergency. Tony was principal at the time. He took over my class so that I could get son to the hospital immediately. His motto was "your family first, then the Schoenly family (our school) next."

A special acknowledgment to my beta readers, Cheryl, Carol Ann, Gail, and Robert who read and reread so many of my pieces and whose words of encouragement provided support throughout my journey.

Lastly, thank you to Rebel Books Press, who published "The Wednesday Lady."

Printed in the USA
CPSIA information can be obtained
at www.ICGtesting.com
LVHW040037010624
781578LV00008BA/682